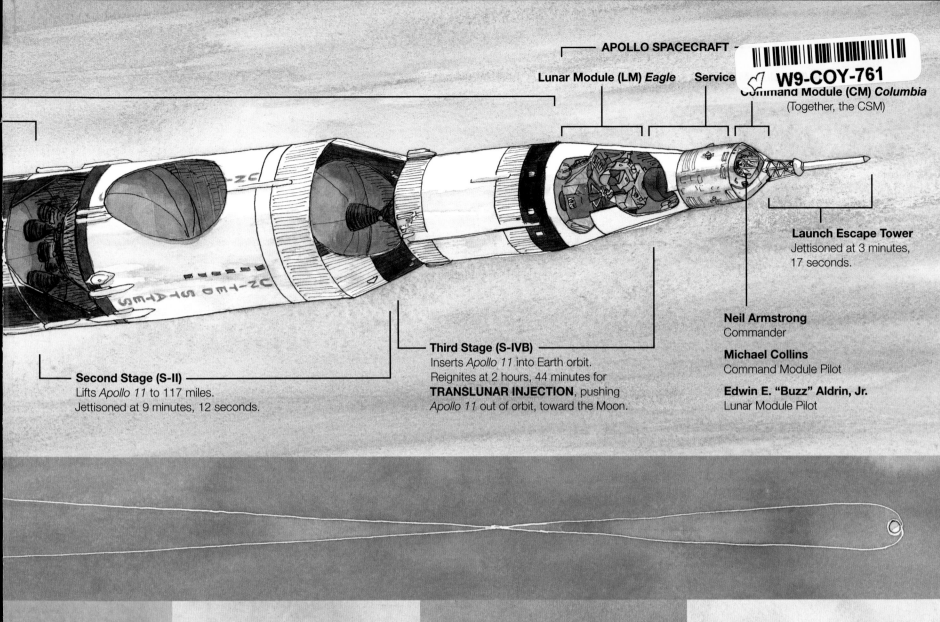

APOLLO SPACECRAFT

Lunar Module (LM) *Eagle*   Service   Command Module (CM) *Columbia*
(Together, the CSM)

Launch Escape Tower
Jettisoned at 3 minutes,
17 seconds.

Second Stage (S-II)
Lifts *Apollo 11* to 117 miles.
Jettisoned at 9 minutes, 12 seconds.

Third Stage (S-IVB)
Inserts *Apollo 11* into Earth orbit.
Reignites at 2 hours, 44 minutes for
TRANSLUNAR INJECTION, pushing
Apollo 11 out of orbit, toward the Moon.

Neil Armstrong
Commander

Michael Collins
Command Module Pilot

Edwin E. "Buzz" Aldrin, Jr.
Lunar Module Pilot

LUNAR LIFTOFF
Armstrong and Aldrin ride
the ascent stage of *Eagle*
up from Tranquility Base at
1:54 PM EDT on July 21.

Back in lunar orbit, the LM and CSM
dock. Armstrong and Aldrin rejoin
Collins in *Columbia*, bringing with them
lunar samples.

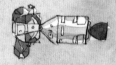

Eagle's ascent stage is then released . . .

. . . and the CSM engine ignites for
TRANSEARTH INJECTION.

After a two-and-a-half-day
TRANSEARTH COAST *Apollo 11*
reaches Earth and jettisons the Service
Module.

ENTRY and LANDING
Columbia enters Earth's atmosphere . . .

. . . and splashes down safely at 12:50 PM
EDT on July 24.

The astronauts are taken by helicopter to the
USS *Hornet*, where they enter the Mobile
Quarantine Facility.

After three weeks in quarantine—and
with no sign of Moon germs—Armstrong,
Collins, and Aldrin are released to parades,
celebrations, and a goodwill tour of the world.

For my parents

SOURCES

Andrew Chaikin's *A Man on the Moon* was, long ago now, my starting point for approaching the subject of the Apollo Moon missions. It is an accessible history of the program, from the fire that claimed the crew of *Apollo 1* to the accomplished lunar geology carried out by the crew of *Apollo 17*, with an emphasis on the experiences of the astronauts. *Carrying the Fire: An Astronaut's Journey* and *Liftoff: The Story of America's Adventure in Space*, both by Michael Collins, the best writer ever to ride a Saturn V, relate the experience of *Apollo 11* and also the broader development of the space program. Norman Mailer's *Of a Fire on the Moon* gives a sense of *Apollo 11* in the context of the 1960s (for much of the book Mailer refers to himself in the third person as Aquarius) and also adroitly explains the mechanics of the flight (Mailer began his undergraduate work at Harvard as a student of aeronautical engineering). *Apollo: The Race to the Moon*, by Charles Murray and Catherine Bly Cox, tells the stories of the engineers who imagined and designed Apollo, and of the flight controllers who ran the missions. Also valuable were *First Man: The Life of Neil A. Armstrong*, by James R. Hansen, and *First on the Moon: A Voyage with Neil Armstrong, Michael Collins, and Edwin E. Aldrin, Jr.*, by Armstrong, Collins, and Aldrin, with Gene Farmer and Dora Jane Hamblin. For readers curious as to how all the pieces fit together in the strange craft of Apollo, *Virtual Apollo* and *Virtual LM*, by Scott P. Sullivan, offer a range of interior and exterior views.

The tremendous amount of diagrams, press releases, photographs, videos, flight plans, and memoranda that NASA makes available to the public were invaluable in the preparation of this book. Places to find them online include NASA's web site at http://spaceflight.nasa.gov/history/apollo/index.html and the Apollo Lunar Surface Journal at http://www.hq.nasa.gov/alsj/.

Useful films about Apollo included the documentaries *In the Shadow of the Moon* and, especially, Al Reinert's *For All Mankind*. The ten-plus hours of footage compiled in *Apollo 11: Men on the Moon*, from Spacecraft Films, might only be for people writing their own books about *Apollo 11*—but if you've got a yen for obscure snippets and real-time footage, this DVD is for you. Dramatizations of the missions, such as *Apollo 13* and the HBO series *From the Earth to the Moon*, had their place, as well. Archival CBS coverage of the landing, which I watched at the Paley Center for Media in New York, gave a sense of the excitement and suspense that attended the first landing. The footage is worth watching just to see Walter Cronkite at a loss for words immediately following the landing; to astronaut Wally Schirra, in the studio to help explain events to the viewers, an almost giddy Cronkite finally says, "Wally, say something."

Finally, visits to the Smithsonian National Air and Space Museum in Washington, DC, and the Johnson Space Center in Houston, Texas, allowed a firsthand look at mission tools, suits, machinery, and what is now known as "historic mission control." The visits also allowed a look at the actual vehicles of Apollo, overwhelming in their intricacy, boldness, and monumentality, and a fitting metaphor for the program as a whole.

FOR THE EXPANDED EDITION

Revisiting *Moonshot* has meant revisiting the above sources and discovering new ones, including the classic *Chariots for Apollo: The NASA History of Manned Lunar Spacecraft to 1969*, by Courtney G. Brooks, James M. Grimwood, and Loyd S. Swenson, Jr., and the more recently published works *Spacesuit: Fashioning Apollo*, by Nicholas de Monchaux, *Hidden Figures: The American Dream and the Untold Story of the Black Women Mathematicians Who Helped Win the Space Race*, by Margot Lee Shetterly, and, online, "The 'Rope Mother' Margaret Hamilton" by Paul Ceruzzi, for the Smithsonian National Air and Space Museum. Recent 3-D scans by the Smithsonian of the interior of the command module *Columbia*—viewable online and through virtual reality apps—improved my sense of the scale and layout of that ship. Also online, the websites listed above are still up, running, and valuable. NASA's site at nasa.gov and the Smithsonian National Air and Space Museum's at airandspace.si.edu are also recommended, and probably easier to navigate, too, for those just starting their own online Apollo research.

In preparing this edition it has been a help and a pleasure to talk with friends who have gone on their own Apollo research journeys, including Sharyn November and John Rocco, and I owe them thanks for their help and encouragement. I am also once again indebted to everyone at Atheneum/Simon & Schuster, especially Michael McCartney and, above all, Richard Jackson. Finally, this edition, like the original, is dedicated to my parents, and I remain grateful for their continued support.

Atheneum Books for Young Readers. An imprint of Simon & Schuster Children's Publishing Division. 1230 Avenue of the Americas, New York, New York 10020. Copyright © 2009 by Brian Floca. All rights reserved, including the right of reproduction in whole or in part in any form. Book design by Brian Floca and Michael McCartney. The text for this book is set in Helvetica Neue. The illustrations for this book are rendered in watercolor, ink, acrylic, and gouache, with some revisions made or incorporated digitally. Manufactured in China. 0119 SCP. First Edition. 10 9 8 7 6 5 4 3 2 1. CIP data for this book is available from the Library of Congress. ISBN 978-1-5344-4030-2 (hc). ISBN 978-1-5344-4051-7 (eBook).

MOONSHOT

THE FLIGHT OF APOLLO 11 · BRIAN FLOCA

EXPANDED FOR THE 50TH ANNIVERSARY OF THE FIRST MOON LANDING

A Richard Jackson Book
Atheneum Books for Young Readers
New York London Toronto Sydney New Delhi

High above
there is the Moon,
cold and quiet,
no air, no life,
but glowing in the sky.

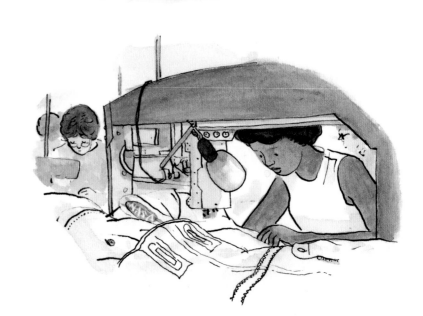

Here below
there are men and women
plotting new paths and drawing new plans.

They are sewing suits, assembling ships,
and writing codes for computers.

Nuts and bolts, needles and thread,
and numbers, numbers, numbers.

Thousands of people,
for millions of parts.

And now here below
there are three men

who close themselves
in those new suits,
who are ready to ride
in those new ships.

They—*click*—lock hands
in heavy gloves,

and—*click*—lock heads
in large, round helmets.

It is summer here in Florida,
hot, and near the sea.
But now these men are dressed
for colder, stranger places.
They walk with stiff and awkward steps
in suits not made for Earth.

They have studied and practiced and trained,
and said good-bye to family and friends.
If all goes well, they will be gone for one week,
gone where no one has been.

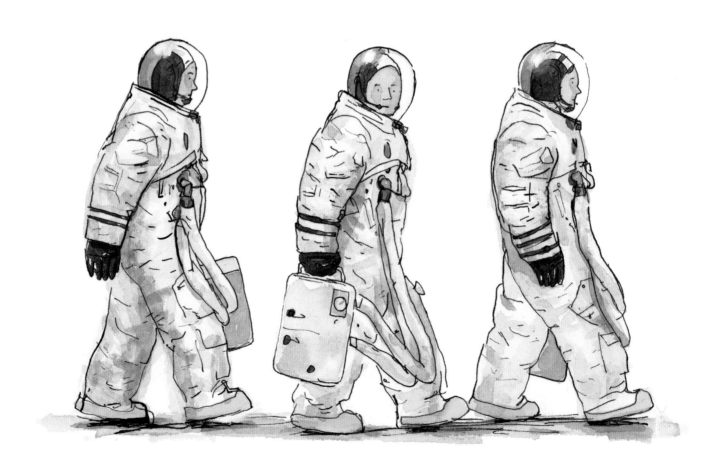

Their two small spaceships are
Columbia and *Eagle*.
They are locked to the top of the rocket
that will lift them into space,
a monster of a machine:
It stands thirty stories,
it weighs six million pounds,
a tower full of fuel and fire
and valves and pipes and engines,
too big to believe, but built to fly—
the mighty, massive Saturn V.

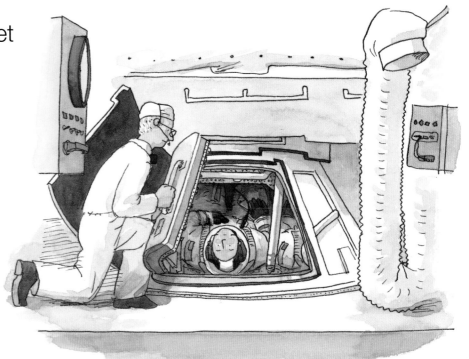

The astronauts squeeze in
to *Columbia*'s sideways seats,
lying on their backs,
facing toward the sky—
Neil Armstrong on the left,
Michael Collins on the right,
Buzz Aldrin in the middle.

Click and they fasten straps.
Clunk and the hatch is sealed.

There they wait,
T-minus two hours,
with the Saturn
humming beneath them.

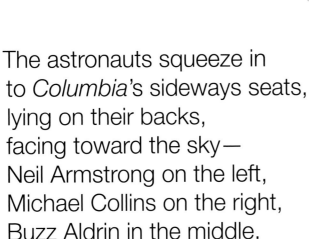

Near the rocket, in Launch Control,
and far away in Houston, in Mission Control,
there are numbers, screens, and charts,
ways of watching and checking
every system and part of *Apollo 11*,
the fuel, the valves, the pipes, the engines,
the beats of the astronauts' hearts.

The hours turn to minutes,
and now the countdown quickens.

Everyone watching is asked the question:
"GO/NO GO?"
And everyone watching answers back:
"GO."
"GO."
"GO."
Apollo 11 is GO for launch.

10...9...8...7...

Ignition sequence started.
Flames push hard against the pad,
every second pushing harder.

6...5...4...

But still the rocket
does not rise.

Mighty arms
hold it steady . . .

hold it till the
countdown's finish . . .

3 . . . 2 . . . 1 . . .

ZERO

LIFTOFF!

The rocket is released!
It rises
foot by foot,
it rises
pound by pound.

It climbs
the summer sky.
It rides a flapping,
cracking flame
and shakes the air,
and shakes the earth,
and makes a mighty

ROAR.

Armstrong, Collins, Aldrin
ride the fire and thunder
pressed in their seats,
their bodies as heavy as clay.

The rocket below them
sheds parts as it soars.
Bolts explode, engines ignite—
first stage, second stage, escape tower—
gone!

The rocket flies lighter,
the rocket flies faster;
in twelve minutes' time,
it's one hundred miles high.

Then, after an orbit around the Earth
to talk with Mission Control
to check the course
and the rocket and ships,
the rocket's last stage fires again,
pushing the astronauts on.

And when the Earth
has rolled beneath
and rolled behind
and let the astronauts go,
the Saturn's last stage opens wide
and releases *Columbia*,
the small, silver ship
that sat at the top
of the rocket.

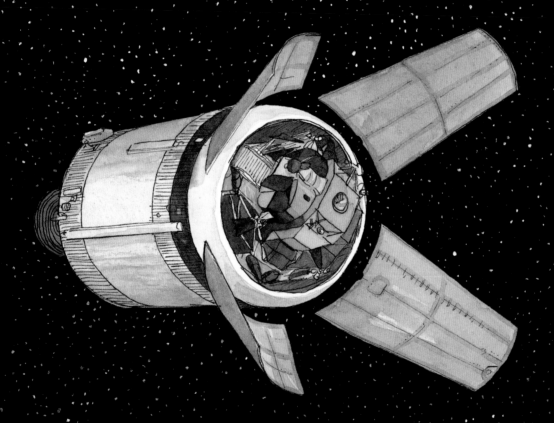

And here, hidden till now, is *Eagle*, too,
a stranger ship, more bug than bird,
a black and gold and folded spider.

Michael Collins, *Columbia*'s pilot,
turns her back around,
points her toward the *Eagle* . . .

. . . and locks the ships together.

Then Armstrong, Collins, Aldrin
leave the last of the Saturn
and travel on in their
two small ships,
joined together,
flown as one.

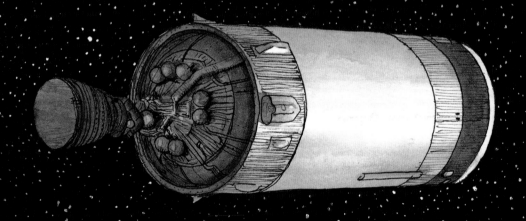

They go rushing into darkness,
flying toward the Moon,
far away,
cold and quiet,
no air, no life,
but glowing in the sky.

Onboard *Columbia* and *Eagle*,
Armstrong, Collins, Aldrin
un*click* gloves,
un*click* helmets,
un*click* the straps
that hold them down,
and float inside their small ships,
their home for a week.

Here there is no up or down;
an astronaut can spin in air and
turn a floor into a wall
or a ceiling to a floor.

On those ceilings, walls, and floors,
there are straps and screens and gauges,
buttons, handles, hoses,
and switches, switches, switches.

There are food and clothes
packed into corners,
and flight plans, flashlights,
pens, and cameras—and they float, too.
They drift from hands and pockets.
(That's why there's Velcro everywhere:
for holding things so they stay put.)

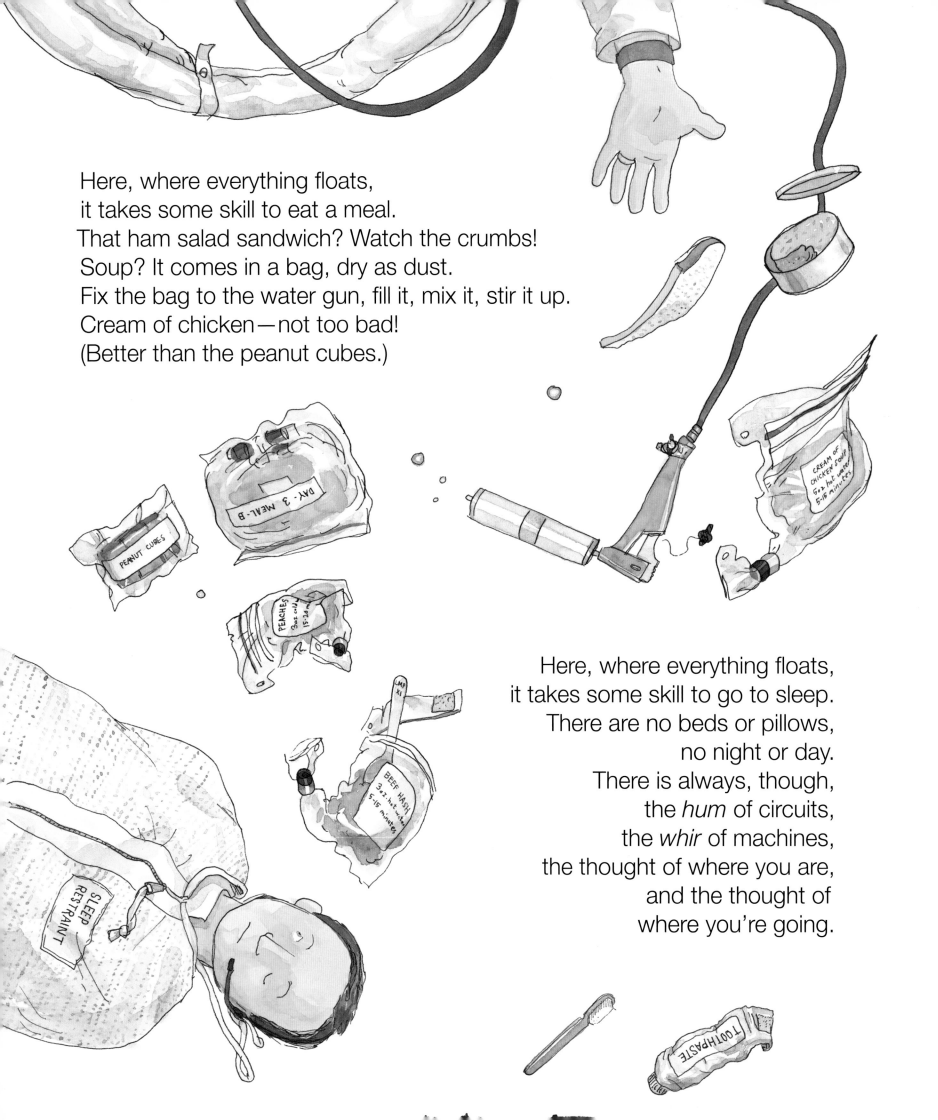

Here, where everything floats,
it takes some skill to eat a meal.
That ham salad sandwich? Watch the crumbs!
Soup? It comes in a bag, dry as dust.
Fix the bag to the water gun, fill it, mix it, stir it up.
Cream of chicken—not too bad!
(Better than the peanut cubes.)

Here, where everything floats,
it takes some skill to go to sleep.
There are no beds or pillows,
no night or day.
There is always, though,
the *hum* of circuits,
the *whir* of machines,
the thought of where you are,
and the thought of
where you're going.

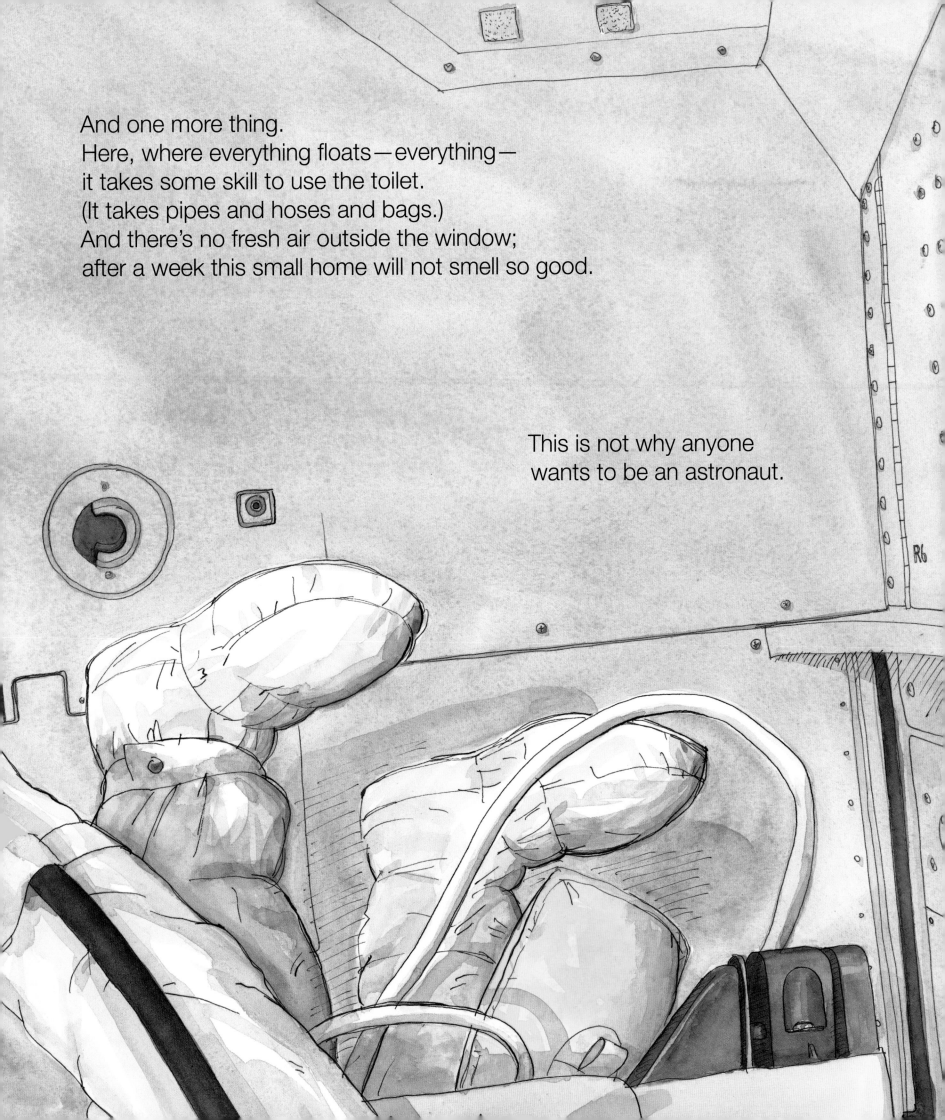

And one more thing.
Here, where everything floats—everything—
it takes some skill to use the toilet.
(It takes pipes and hoses and bags.)
And there's no fresh air outside the window;
after a week this small home will not smell so good.

This is not why anyone
wants to be an astronaut.

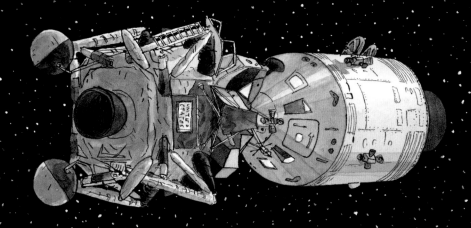

But still ahead
there is the Moon,
    cold and quiet,
    no air, no life,
    but glowing in the sky.
    Glowing and growing,
    it takes them in,
    it pulls them close.

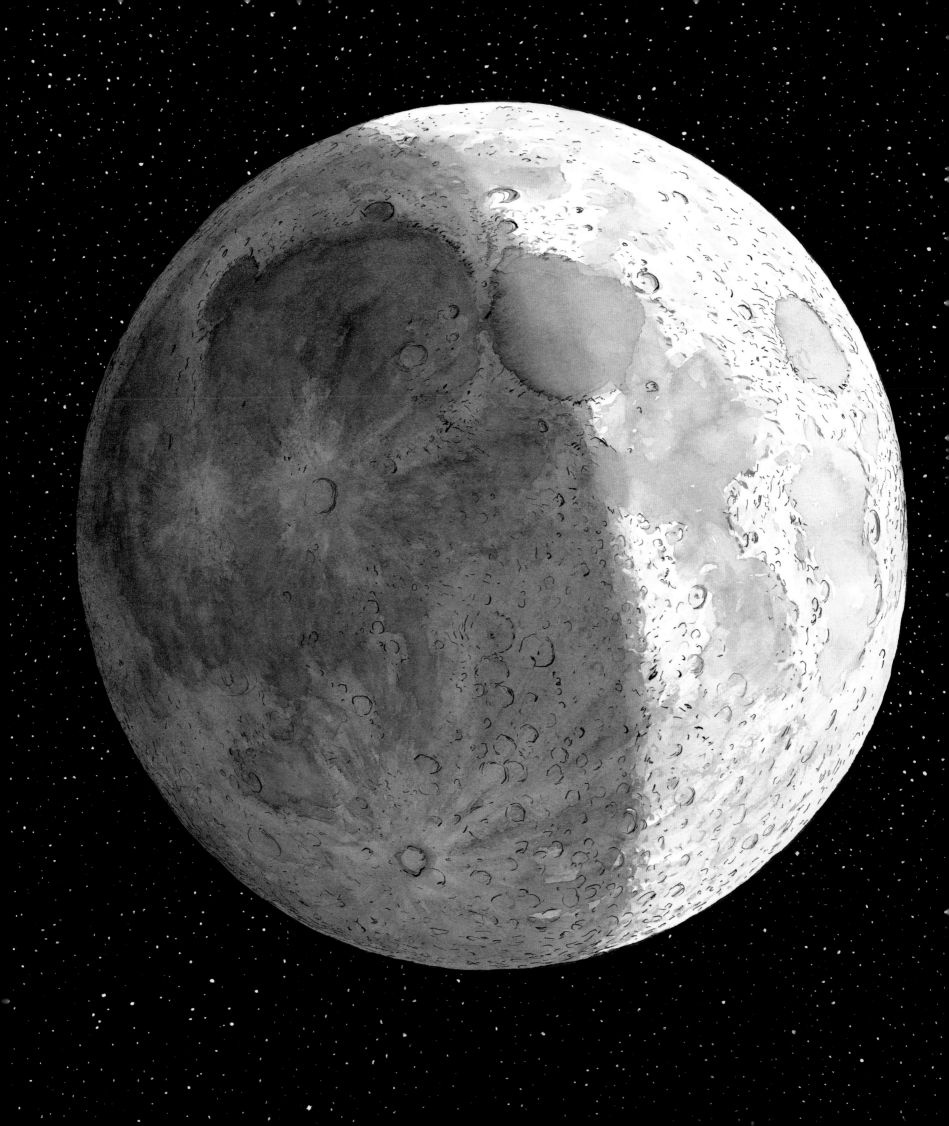

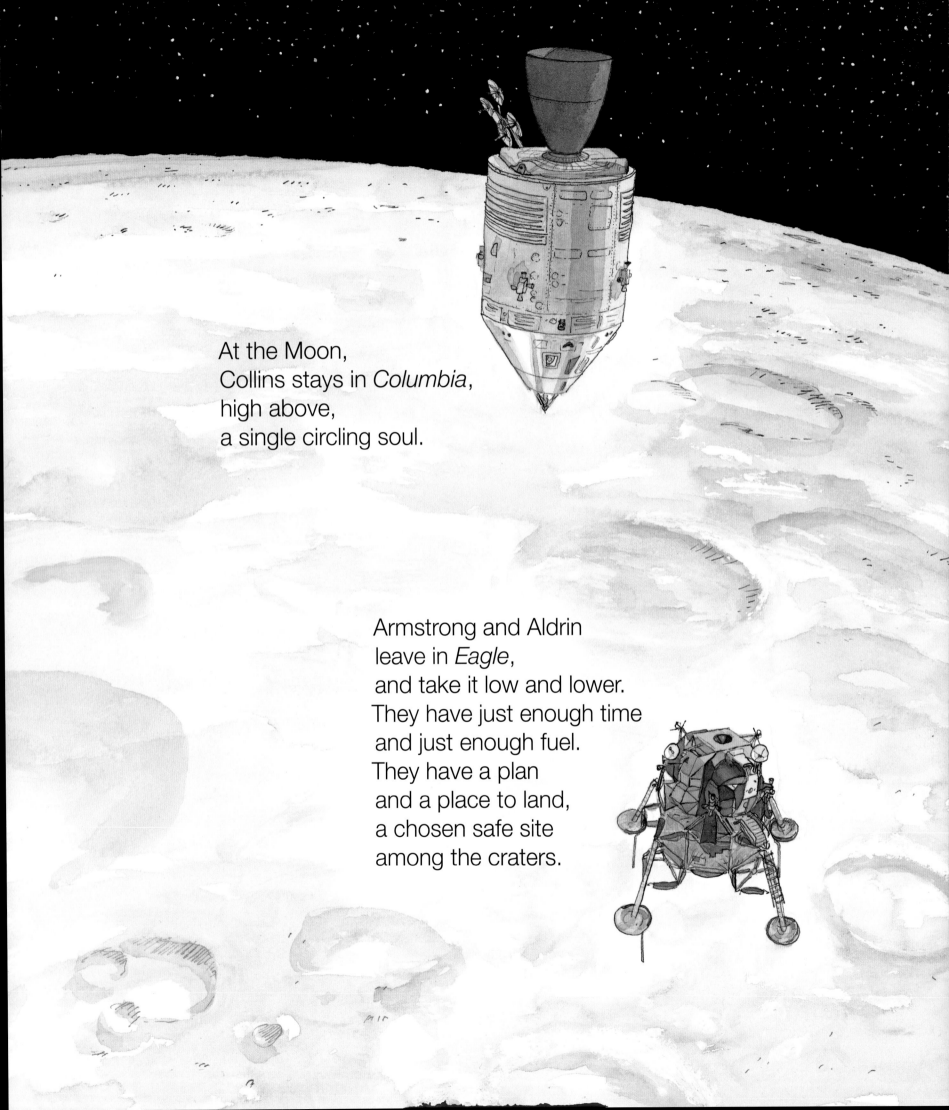

At the Moon,
Collins stays in *Columbia*,
high above,
a single circling soul.

Armstrong and Aldrin
leave in *Eagle*,
and take it low and lower.
They have just enough time
and just enough fuel.
They have a plan
and a place to land,
a chosen safe site
among the craters.

Now friends and strangers
in the distance, down below,
stay up late, get up early,
and stop as one
to watch and wait.
There are only maps and models to see;
there is no camera that can show
the landing far away.

But what strange sounds there are to *hear*!
Whistles, beeps, and static,
weird new words and
quick, clipped news
of altitudes and speeds,
leaping across the dark
between Mission Control and the men
who are taking the *Eagle* to land on the Moon,
who are going where no one has been.

Onboard *Eagle*,
Aldrin calls out information
while Armstrong steers the ship.
They fly lower and lower, looking,
looking for their landing site.
But now *Eagle*, they see, has flown too far.
They are miles from where they mean to be,
and below their small and spindly ship
they see no level place,
only broken stone and rock,
only shadows in deep craters
on the great and growing Moon.

And inside *Eagle*, alarms light up—
warnings that come in numbers and codes
not even the astronauts know.
But GO, GO, says Mission Control:
"*Eagle*, Houston. You're GO for landing."

Far from home and far from help,
still steady, steady the astronauts fly,
as time and fuel are running out.

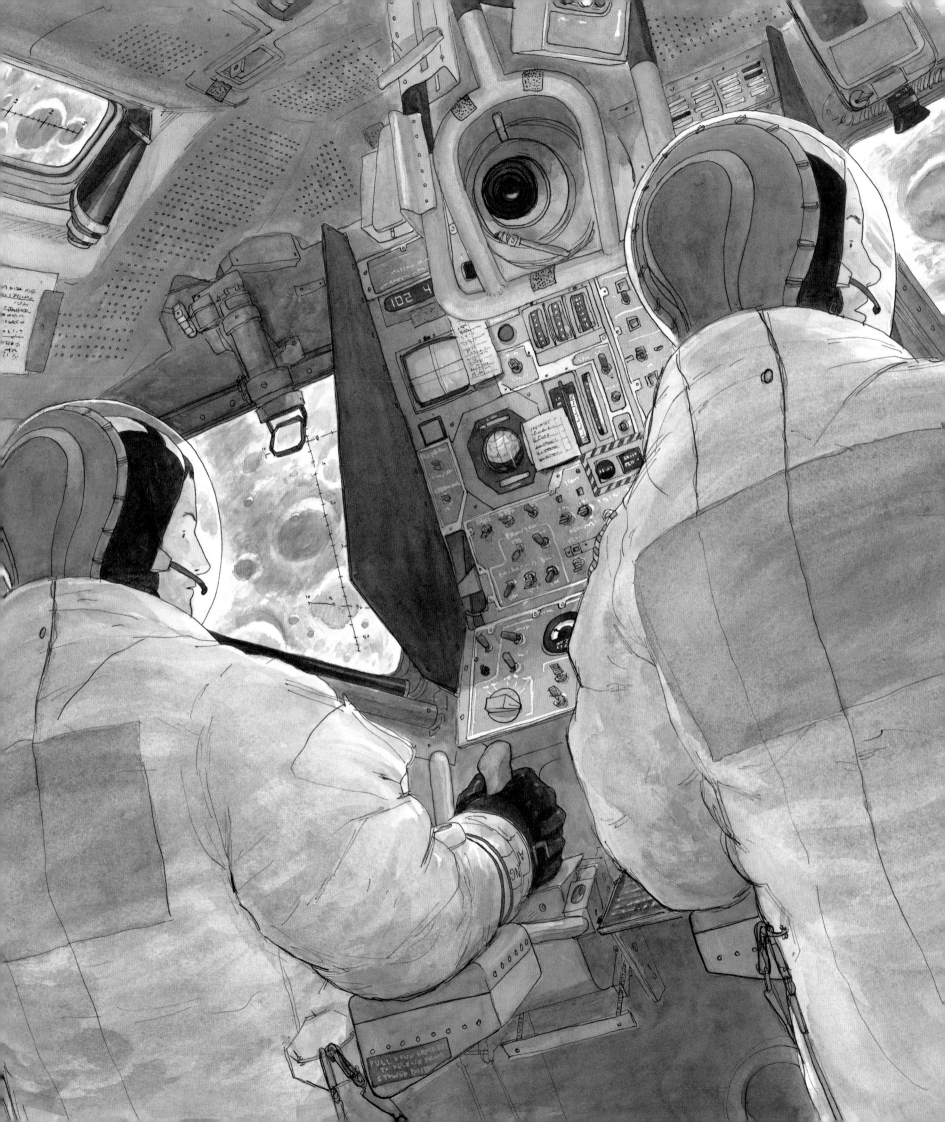

Then . . . there! Clean and flat, not too far!
Sixty seconds left! Armstrong fires the rockets.
Eagle slows and lower goes until a spray of dust,
a bloom of moon, flowers up around her.
Slow and slower,
low and lower,
low and lower—
landing!

And far away,
where friends and strangers lean to listen,
where friends and strangers lean to hear,
there comes a distant voice:
Armstrong, calling from the Moon,
calm as a man who just parked a car.
"Houston," he says. "Tranquility Base here. The *Eagle* has landed."

Armstrong is calm—but on Earth they cheer!

Then Armstrong and Aldrin
climb down from the *Eagle*
in heavy gloves, in large, round helmets,
in suits not made for Earth—

—in suits made for the Moon,
here below, all around them,
cold and quiet,
no air, but *life*—
there is life
on the strange and silent,
magnificent Moon.

Armstrong and Aldrin
walk its rough, wide places.
They step, they hop.
As light as boys,
they lope, they leap!

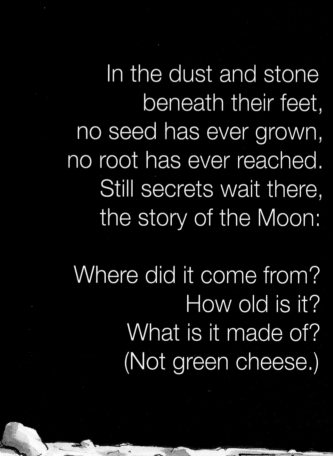

In the dust and stone
beneath their feet,
no seed has ever grown,
no root has ever reached.
Still secrets wait there,
the story of the Moon:

Where did it come from?
How old is it?
What is it made of?
(Not green cheese.)

In the sky above their heads,
the sun is strong and shining—
this is *daytime*, here on the Moon.
It doesn't look like a day back home;
without any air to scatter the light
and make sky turn blue,
the view from here is straight into space,
and the sky is a bottomless black.

Bottomless black,
without even stars to see,
for the light is so bright,
shining down from the sun,
bouncing up off the Moon,
that the stars are outshone,
and all of them stay hidden.

But in that black and starless sky . . .

. . . high above
there is the Earth,
rushing oceans, racing clouds,
swaying fields and forests.
Family, friends, and strangers,
everyone you've ever known,
everyone you might—
the good and lonely Earth,
glowing in the sky.

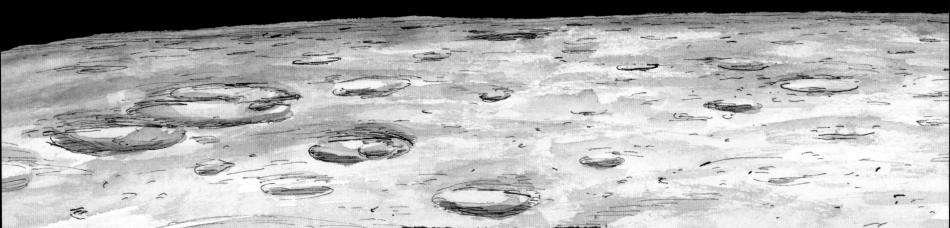

Now it's midnight in Houston, at Mission Control,
and that's how it feels to the astronauts, too.
(And what time is it, here on the Moon? That's a harder question.)

Armstrong and Aldrin climb back into *Eagle*.
It's time to sleep, or at least to try,
but it's cold here in *Eagle*,
and it's crowded, and loud,
and now *Eagle*'s air is full of dust—
full of the dust of the Moon!
It was carried in on suits and boots,
and now it gets in the astronauts' noses.
(It smells like damp ashes, like a fire put out.)

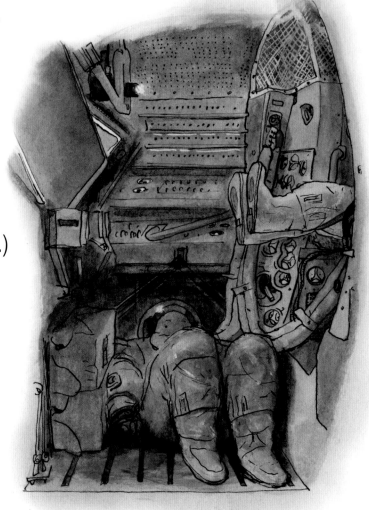

The astronauts keep their helmets on
to keep from breathing in dust.
Armstrong climbs up on the engine,
and Aldrin curls up on the floor.
(The *Eagle* was not built for comfort.)

It is not a good night's sleep—
it is barely even rest!

Still, the hours go by, and then rested or not, it's time to go.

Eagle's landing stage becomes a launch pad,
and 3 . . . 2 . . .1 . . . Armstrong and Aldrin fly the top of the *Eagle*
up, up, up from the Moon—their second liftoff of the trip.

High above the Moon, *Columbia* is waiting:
Columbia and *Eagle*, two small ships
(and *Eagle* smaller than she was before).
They dance, they spin, closer and closer,
until Collins can dock and lock them together.
Two small ships, flown as one again.

Then hatches open, and *hello!*

Three astronauts,
together again, too,
successful and happy,
Armstrong, Collins, Aldrin.

They leave the last of the *Eagle* behind them
and fly together from the Moon,
which rolls beneath,
which rolls behind,
letting them loose,
letting them go.

They carry pictures,
stones, and stories,
and a view of home,
seen from far away.

They fly together,
two and a half
more days in space.

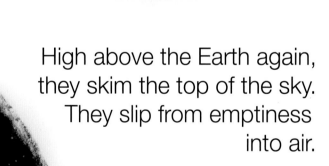

High above the Earth again,
they skim the top of the sky.
They slip from emptiness
into air.

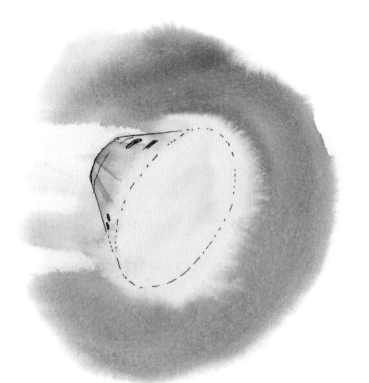

They are flying, more like *falling*,
diving down to the world below,
flying, falling, *fast*—
four hundred miles every minute!

Falling, *fast*,
but now pushing on air,
and using the air
and the shape of their ship
to slow down.

Pushing on air,
cutting down speed,
building up pressure, and building up *heat*!
Hot and then hotter, until flame, until fire!

Now protected by shields,
pressed again in their seats,
the astronauts ride as a glow grows around them.

They cross the sky like a torch,
trailing a blazing tail.

Then
drogue chutes,
pilot chutes,
main chutes—
OPEN!

The parachutes catch the air,
the parachutes catch the sky,
they slow *Columbia*'s fall.

Now slower,
now safely,
now swinging,
now drifting,
low and lower,
in the last small
piece of *Apollo 11,*
Armstrong,
Collins,
and Aldrin
return.

Back to family,
back to friends,
to warmth,
to light,
to trees
and blue water.
Back from the Moon,
    they land with a

SPLASH!

To warmth,
to light,
to home at last.

ONE GIANT LEAP

"First, I believe that this nation should commit itself to achieving the goal, before this decade is out, of landing a man on the Moon and returning him safely to the Earth."

So President John F. Kennedy stated his goals for the United States in space in May of 1961. The Moon was an ambitious target for a country that could not yet lift an astronaut into orbit around the Earth, but Kennedy had his reasons for the choice. In the new race to explore space, the United States had found itself, again and again, squarely behind the achievements of the Soviet Union. Eager to catch up and move ahead, Kennedy had searched for an achievement that would be important to exploration, that would make an impression, and that the United States had a fighting chance of accomplishing first. Advisors let him know the Soviets would have a clear lead in certain efforts, some of which might have seemed like logical next steps in space exploration, such as putting space stations in orbit above Earth. But there were other goals, they told him, further out, that would give the United States a chance for a first—including a trip to the Moon.

But how to do it, and how to do it in just nine years? Serious advocates of space exploration and pulp science fiction alike (and Hergé's Tintin adventure *Destination Moon*, too) had made familiar the image of a rocket standing on its tail fins on the lunar surface, ready to return, whole, to Earth. The great problem with this approach, though, would be weight, and not just the weight of the rocket, but also of the fuel it would require to travel, intact, to and from the Moon.

Faced with limits of time and technology, engineers instead began to imagine reaching the Moon with multiple smaller, lighter, and specialized craft: a Command Module and a Service Module (together, the CSM) and, for the actual landing of astronauts on the Moon, a Lunar Excursion Module. (The name was later simplified to Lunar Module, or LM; "Excursion" was thought to sound too casual.) These small ships would be lifted into space by a dedicated launch vehicle, the Saturn V rocket. The Saturn V would by necessity still be enormous, and heavy, but would diminish in size and weight as it went, dismantling itself as it flew. It would take the dedicated effort of over 400,000 men and women, working at companies and universities across the country, to turn these ideas into a built, functioning reality. The result was the incredible shrinking *Apollo 11*, a fantastically complicated assembly of machinery and systems that left Earth the size of a skyscraper—363 feet in height, almost six and a half million pounds in weight—and returned the size of a Volkswagen bus.

Apollo 11's remarkable feats of disassembly began just two minutes after it lifted off from Cape Kennedy, Florida, on the morning of July 16, 1969. In that short time, the Saturn V lifted the CSM *Columbia*, LM *Eagle*, and astronauts Neil Armstrong, Michael Collins, and Edwin "Buzz" Aldrin, Jr., forty miles into the sky. The rocket's gigantic first-stage booster tank, its fuel spent, was then released by explosive bolts and sent tumbling into the Atlantic Ocean. The second stage then burned for six minutes, pushing *Apollo 11* to roughly one hundred twenty miles above the Earth, before that stage, too, was jettisoned. A firing of the third stage placed the rocket in orbit around the Earth. A little over two hours later, after a review by the crew and Mission Control, a second firing of the third stage pushed *Apollo 11* out of Earth orbit and toward the Moon.

Shortly afterward, *Columbia* separated from Saturn's third stage. The panels that made up the cone of the third stage then parted like so many petals, exposing the *Eagle*. Michael Collins, *Columbia*'s pilot, docked the two ships and pulled the *Eagle* free. Now the Saturn V's work was finished; *Columbia* and *Eagle* left it behind and continued on their own.

As they left Earth orbit the astronauts were moving at a speed of 25,000 miles an hour—almost seven miles a second—but like a ball thrown high into the air, *Apollo 11* still felt the tug of Earth's gravity. For roughly 200,000 miles it pulled on them, reducing their speed, finally, to some 2,000 miles per hour. At about 40,000 miles from the Moon, though, the astronauts entered the lunar sphere of influence; now they were pulled forward by the Moon, rather than back by the Earth, and they gained speed again. On July 19 the crew fired *Columbia*'s bell engine in the direction of their flight, dampening that speed sufficiently to be captured by the Moon's gravity and to enter lunar orbit.

The next day, Armstrong and Aldrin began the descent to their landing site in *Eagle*. Up to this point, the crew of *Apollo 11* had traveled paths tested on previous missions: *Apollo 8* had first left Earth to orbit the Moon; *Apollo 9* had first tested and rendezvoused Command and Lunar Modules; and the crew of *Apollo 10* had flown to the Moon and then taken their LM to within nine miles of its surface. One step had led to the next. Now the final task fell to *Apollo 11*: to set a strange new ship on a strange new world—to land on the Moon.

The flight down was not smooth. There were communication glitches, obscurely coded computer alarms, errors in *Eagle*'s course (the ship ended up four miles downrange from its intended landing site), and, finally, the threat of low fuel and of a late, dangerous abort to the flight. The astronauts and Mission Control handled it all with trademark cool, but there was palpable relief in the voice of Mission Control communications officer (and astronaut) Charlie Duke when he got the news that *Eagle* was safely landed at the Sea of Tranquility: "Roger, Tranquility, we copy you on the ground," he replied. "You got a bunch of guys about to turn blue. We're breathing again. Thanks a lot."

Six hours after the landing, Armstrong and Aldrin were ready to step onto the Moon. A camera attached to the side of *Eagle* beamed shadowy images of Armstrong's climb down *Eagle*'s ladder back to Earth—and Earth was watching. Six hundred million people—one out of every five people alive—watched Armstrong set foot onto the lunar surface, remarking as he did,